Vision Boarding The Faith-Based Way

How To Activate Your Dreams

By Nancy Gathecha

ISBN-10: 1981813381
ISBN-13: 978-1981813384

Published by Naga Publishing
Postfach 7586
53075
Bonn, Germany

www.NagaPublishing.com

DEDICATIONS

To the Giver of dreams, the Source of purpose-led vision, You are the Author and Finisher of our faith.

To my role model, your legacy of faith lives on and the seeds you sowed continue to bear fruit. Thank you, Maptsa.

To all visionaries,

"Keep your dreams alive. Understand to achieve anything requires faith and belief in yourself, vision, hard work, determination, and dedication. Remember all things are possible for those who believe." - Gail Devers

CONTENTS

INTRODUCTION

"The only thing worse than being blind is having sight, but no vision. "- Helen Keller

Congratulations! You've taken a bold step towards making your life and business dreams a reality. The fact that you're reading this book indicates that you're a fellow visionary; a man or woman of faith who takes action.

Do you have a dormant vision or unfulfilled desires? Great! Because I wrote this book with you in mind. To support you with a faith-based tool that not only gives you practical strategies on vision-casting, but also clarifies questions about the place vision boards, and the Law of Attraction have in a believer's life. Your big dreams can become a reality, and this book shows you how to activate them so that you go from dreaming to doing so that you achieve your potential. Let me explain why and how vision boarding will help you achieve your intentions faster.

Did you know in its natural habitat, the African impala can jump over 10 feet and cover a distance of over 30 feet? But the same animal when kept in a zoo will not jump over the 3-foot tall wall surrounding it.

Why won't the African Impala jump?

These agile animals will not jump the wall unless they can see where their feet will land. So even though they have the potential to escape the zoo, they remain trapped inside because the wall obstructs their sight. With no vision beyond the physical barrier, they do not leap into the freedom that's available. And so their potential is not unleashed.

And so it is with us sometimes. Although we have the potential to live the big God-given dreams inside us, like the African Impala we do not take a leap of faith because we can not "see" where we are going to land. Real obstacles and imaginary walls in our minds obstruct us, and we remain stuck and unfulfilled in the zoos of life.

But if you are ready to break out of confinement, vision boarding can help you push through visible and invisible barriers helping you take inspired action to have, be or do what we are already wired to achieve.

By the time you finish this book, you'll be ready to take inspired action steps towards your vision. Because just as the African Impala is wired to jump, you too have been wired with leaping potential to fulfill the dormant dreams inside you.

I'll be using the words vision and dreams interchangeably, but implying the same thing - unfulfilled desires to have, be, or do something. And while it's OK to want beautiful houses, cars, and holidays, this book goes beyond acquiring the material trappings money can buy and addressing eternal purpose, fulfillment, and the God equation.

Many believers often want to take an either/or stand, implying you can't be wealthy and serve God at the same time. But it's possible to love God and also enjoy material prosperity. Being wealthy is not evil as long as we do not serve the God of money - mammon and love earthly possessions like the rich young ruler in Mark 10:17-27. Jesus said it is hard for the wealthy to enter heaven. Hard, but not impossible with God. The last part of that verse implies with God it IS possible for a rich man to enter heaven.

In case you don't believe in God or the Bible, allow me to make a quick note about the Bible references you'll find in this book. I respect your choice of beliefs and by no means exclude you in any way. Instead, I invite you to read this with an open heart because I too used to be an atheist. More on that later. But for now, know vision-boarding will work for you irrespective of what you choose to believe.

As a born-again believer, I wrote this faith-based book with a biblical approach on how to activate your big God-given dreams using a purpose-led vision board. Because you and I know it takes money to build a dream, it behooves us to adopt the mindset that spirituality and wealth are possible, instead of the "either riches or God" mindset. Whether you are starting afresh or already working on your dreams, vision-boarding will help you accelerate your success.

You've probably heard of vision boards from The Secret or some New Age concept, here's my full disclosure; I've never actually read that book. But I've watched enough videos and read articles about the Law of Attraction. Being a curious researcher by default, when I find something interesting, I go beyond the surface of theories and principles. Not to unearth anything new, but to understand how and why something works.

The Bible says there's nothing new under the sun, and in many (not all) New Age teachings, the wisdom and timeless principles originated from God. But secular people unknowingly, or conveniently leave Him out, twist or pervert the information. As you read this book, you will discover that vision boarding is in and of itself not a bad thing. In fact, you'll be surprised to learn that it's a powerful biblical principle, but we Christians shun it because we don't want to dabble in anything that's not of God.

But did you know the Law of Attraction theory is similar to a biblical principle based on the verse, *"As he thinks in his heart, so is he."* (Proverbs 23:7)? Our thoughts become things. What we constantly think about, we eventually bring about. That's because human beings are wonderfully and fearfully created. We're not products of the big bang, and the "Universe" is not a person. Even scientists reach a dead-end with their evolution theory. God is a Spirit, and He created us in His image – you and I are spirits having a human experience on earth.

Despite the faith-based angle, this is neither a theological thesis nor some veiled approval of New Age practices. It's a tool with information I vastly researched and compiled based on scriptural principles, scientific findings, results of my coaching clients, and personal experiences as a Christian. This book is not supposed to be the "gospel truth" about vision boards. I am human, and I miss it because just like you, I'm also a work-in-progress, growing in every aspect.

I invite you to be like the Bereans in Acts 17 who *"received the word with all readiness, and searched the Scriptures daily to find out whether these things were so."* Feel free to read, check, test, examine and correct what I have researched and compiled here.

In the course of my research, I've come across amazing believers who are also scientists. One woman whose work was crucial in answering questions about the science of thought is Dr. Caroline Leaf, a cognitive neuroscientist, who is also born-again. Feel free to Google her for profound insights about secular Law of Attraction versus how science confirms scripture when it comes to our mindset. Her research includes topics relating to optimal brain performance like stress, toxic thoughts, learning, male/female brain differences, and other fascinating studies.

As a life-long learner committed to personal development and growing in faith, am continually researching the topics of mindset, vision, success, and goal-setting. That's why my content also includes practical aspects of productivity. Thessalonians 5:21 says, *"Test everything; hold on to the good."* So instead of throwing the baby out with the bath-water, why not prayerfully read with an open heart, then take what works for you and do something with it.

See I don't believe you're reading this book by coincidence. I imagine like many visionaries you also have dormant or unfulfilled desires.

Something that tugs at your heart on those days when you briefly allow yourself to dream.

Something so big you know it's only possible with faith in God.

Something you desire to have, be or do in this lifetime.

Something beyond the new car, bigger house, or the additional zero at the end of your bank balance.

Why do I believe that about you?

Simple. Because deep inside, each of us wants to feel that we made a difference. That our being on earth mattered and we lived a life of purpose. We long to be part of a bigger picture. To have a reason to excitedly jump out of bed in the morning before the alarm goes off. You and I both know there's more to life besides working to pay the bills, taking an occasional holiday and buying more stuff.

Now don't get me wrong, I believe we should enjoy the fruits of our labor. Like you, I also like shopping, holidays and a beautiful home. But when the toy box of stuff is full, material things alone can feel pretty unfulfilling don't you agree? You're probably reading this book because for starters; you want to activate your personal and professional dreams. A valid reason because God not only deposits those dreams in our hearts, but He also equips us with the potential to achieve them.

However, if beyond the material stuff, deep inside you desire to accomplish something that will benefit someone else, that my friend is a purpose-led vision. I call it big picture dreaming, and it sets the stage for a fulfilling life and holistic success. But if right about now, you feel a slight disconnect because you haven't given much thought to this "big picture" business, relax and read on because we talk about your purpose-led vision in chapter 2.

A common theme I see when working with coaching clients is the desire for meaning and purpose. Many want to "find" their purpose, likes it's a lost item outside themselves, buried somewhere in the Sahara desert. But purpose is an internal thing.

Just like everything manufactured comes perfectly assembled to fulfill the reason it was created, it is with you. When God created you, He wired purpose inside you and the potential to complete an assignment explicitly pre-ordained for you in His big picture.

Just like every puzzle piece has a place in a picture, so too it is with you, you're not an accident, an afterthought, or an imitation of someone else. You're as unique as your fingerprints, and there's a unique role for you in this beautiful experience we call life on earth. As Mark twain said, *"The two most important days in your life are the day you are born and the day you find out why."* Your purpose is your WHY.

It is written in Ephesians 2:10 says that we *were created for good works, which God prepared beforehand that we should walk in.* Our task in life is not to wander aimlessly trying to find a purpose that's somewhere external, but rather to discover, develop and live what's already inside us. We do this by liaising with the Maker and reading His manual. You'd be surprised to learn all that God covers in His word. There are answers for everything that pertains to life and godliness.

Your purpose may be buried deep under the piles of the 9-5 routines or lost in the rate race of life. But it's there, waiting to be discovered and lived. In this book, I show you how activating your dormant dreams can be the catalyst for living your purpose and escaping the rat race of life.

If you implement what you read, by the time you finish this book, you'll have designed an inspiring, beautiful purpose-led vision board. A visual that gives you big picture clarity while motivating you to take daily actions that accelerate your success. And just like success is a journey, living your purpose and dreams is not a one-time event, it's an ongoing process that we grow into as we take steps of faith.

As you read, you'll notice I share examples, and sometimes seem to repeat myself, saying the same thing differently. The repetition is by design. To demonstrate the practical side of this book. The goal is to go beyond theory and show you tried and tested principles that bring results. What's possible for many others including me, is also possible for you.

Because vision-boarding is not a passive concept, you'll get the maximum value from this book if you implement what you read chapter by chapter. We learn and internalize things better when we interact with the content. That's why I created a simple bonus resource to help you implement what you read, so that you get your results faster. Before you read any further, I invite you to first download your free workbook and complimentary quick-start video at www.DesignYourVisionBoard.com

If you prefer to dive straight into the *how-to* of creating your vision board, chapter five is where the action is. Otherwise, let's start at the beginning and look at the *why* and *what* of vision boarding, before addressing the creative *how-to*.

You don't have to remain trapped in the zoos of life like a vision-less Impala. If you're willing to take leaps of faith, your dormant dreams can come alive. Question is, are you ready to overcome physical and mental obstacles?

If your answer is a resounding yes, then read on, because I wrote this book to inspire you to leap over visible and invisible walls.

Thank you for allowing me to be part of your journey with this book. I'd love to connect and hear about your dreams and vision board, so feel free to reach out on my website or on social media. (Preferably Facebook or Instagram).

OK let's get started with why vision boards work.

CHAPTER 1

WHY VISION BOARDING WORKS

"Where there is no vision the people perish."
- Proverbs 28:19

One of the reasons many people meander through life with no purpose and focus is for lack of vision. Like ships without a captain, many arrive at harbors they never intended to be destinations. Sadly, others ship-wreck as the inevitable storms of life toss them to and fro.

While having a vision doesn't guarantee a storm-free life, it acts as an anchor on those days when we need to stop for a minute to make sense of life's unexpected challenges. Instead of aimlessly drifting to unknown destinations, a vision helps bring stability into our otherwise unpredictable and fast-paced lives. We don't have to live by default, miserable about the status quo with unfulfilled potential like the African Impala trapped in a zoo. A purpose-based vision board can help us live by design.

The New Century Version of Proverbs 28:19 says *"Where there is no word from God, people are uncontrolled."* We don't want to be uncontrolled people, but neither do we want to function like mental institute patients in straight-jackets. Having military-like regiments is not fun. We want to find the right balance, not be control-freaks, obsessing over every detail in our lives. Although activating your dreams and goal setting for success requires a certain level of self-control and focus, it doesn't have to be just dull To-Do lists with tight deadlines.

For many of us visionaries and creative heart-centered entrepreneurs, corporate-like lists can make us feel anxious and restricted. One look at that long dry list with due dates and the feeling of overwhelm kicks in. Uninspired we file it away for *later*. And we both know what "I'll do it later" means? Say hello to procrastination, guilt trips, and feeling stuck.

Yet this traditional way of using corporate Day-Timers, lists, and deadlines is how many of us have been taught to approach vision and goal setting. But before we go further, allow me to share a short personal story to connect activating your dreams with goal-setting.

Back in 2007, I was researching for a book I'd been saying I'll write for years. Up until then, I'd always set New Year's resolutions. You know, those that never make it past February? I was serious about achieving my dream to become a published author but extremely frustrated and confused about why the resolutions didn't seem to work. If you know what am talking about, I hope you get better results with resolutions because mine used to fail miserably.

Year in year out, I did what Einstein called insanity; doing the same thing, but expecting different results. I made well-meaning resolutions hoping to fulfill my dreams but remained perplexed about the little to no progress.

But when I finally discovered the difference between goals and resolutions, all that all changed. As a result of that eureka moment and extensive research, armed with a goal-setting system that included a vision board, I began working on my dreams the right way.

After years of dreaming and failed resolutions, I began doing things differently and saw fast results from my actions. Within six months I had written and self-published my very 1st book! *7 Steps To Success – How To Set and Achieve Your Goals.* The 2nd revised and updated paperback edition will be available in 2018. To get a copy simply go to my website www.nagasuccess.com and click the shop page.

In July 2007 the *write a book dream* was ticked off as done! Full throttle on momentum, two months later I published the second book and had both translated into German.

Now, am not trying to impress you, but to impress upon you that yes, vision-boarding and goal-setting to achieve your big dreams works. But there's a left-brained analytical way to go about it, and there's the right-brained creative and fun way.

See although I'm a get-things-done, action-taking woman, I also love to embrace and nurture my feminine creative energy. But this book is not about me. I just wanted to share that personal story to show you that instead of self-defeating resolutions and dull lists, there's a better way for creative visionaries like us to achieve our God-given dreams faster and with ease.

OK, back to you and how vision boarding can work for you. When it comes to activating dreams and goal-setting, we can use both the analytical and creative approach. One way to do this is by designing an inspiring visual of your desires, then setting intentions to achieve those desires. You've probably heard the quote *goals are dreams with deadlines*, but often dreaming is where many of us sabotage our success. We think it's a waste of time and dive right into the goal-setting.

But before you embark on any journey, you need to first get clear on the desired destination. Allowing yourself to day-dream could very well be the missing key in your success equation. And that's what vision boarding is all about. It's about giving yourself permission to first envision your desired goal, then embark on a journey to do what it takes, so that what you see internally, manifests externally.

Instead of working on your intentions with a dry calendar, restrictive spreadsheets, and intimidating deadlines, vision boards give you the freedom to activate your dreams creatively. They're a fun way to achieve the success you desire faster.

If you already like this idea of a productive process you'll enjoy, read on because later you'll see just how well all this works when it comes to using the three main styles of learning - auditory, visual and kinesthetic. Include writing things down by hand, and reading out loud and you have a powerful tool to work with when vision-boarding.

Enough theory, let's get practical here for a moment. Without over-analyzing, consider the next two examples of some common personal and professional dreams and see what inspires you most.

This:

- Lose 10 kilos by 30/6/20
- Write my 1st book by 30/12/2020
- Go on family holiday by 7/9/2019
- Get married by the time I'm 30 years old
- Go on a missions trip to Kenya by 1/1/2024
- Start my online business by 8/8/2018

Or this:

Mind you, I'm not knocking to-do lists and deadlines, if they work for you, great! But why not get the best of both worlds, using both left and right brain thinking by combining visuals and lists?

I work with a vision board, but I'm also a die-hard fan of lists and planning to get things done. The hot-pink girly Filofax I work with has decorated inserts and color-coded dividers. Sometimes I just play with stickers and washi tape while planning and scheduling serious things like taxes and revenue goals.

Because our feelings play a huge role in whether we achieve something or not, if you don't feel happy and excited about a project you're working on, chances are high you won't follow through. You'll put things off, self-sabotage, or give up quickly at the first sign of a challenge. But instead of feeling stressed about unpleasant tasks, (like taxes), when we enjoy the process we fast-track productivity and procrastinate less.

Yet most goal-setting programs only focus on the result you want with no place for emotions. And while that may work for a business plan, for many of us creatives, it's not the best way to stay motivated day in and day out. Feelings may be fickle, but they affect our persistence and productivity. Activating and living your dreams is not a one-time destination, but a journey of growth, why not enjoy the process?

When we don't associate projects with negative stress, we're more inclined to get things done with ease. Goal setting then isn't as intimidating because were are internally inspired. And that's exactly what vision boarding does. It brings an element of fun and motivation to otherwise serious work.

Ideally a beautiful visual should make you feel

excited about activating your dreams with corresponding goals. I don't know about you, but looking at deadlines void of creativity paralyzes me. If I look at the date alone, it intimidates me. My mind begins playing tricks on me with questions like;

Where do I start?

How will I ever get all this done?

What if I don't make the deadline?

When we get into analysis paralysis and decision fatigue we procrastinate. Our good intentions are hijacked by thoughts like, "*Lemme quickly check into Facebook,*" or "*I wonder what's on TV today.*" And you know how that often ends. Hours later, after aimless scrolling or channel flipping, the guilt sets in.

But instead of feeling anxious as you stare at dry lists and restrictive deadlines, a vision board will serve as an inspiring catalyst for action. Then you can always scroll your social media feed or, binge watch your favorite show as a reward after getting something done.

What's Your Why?

Vision boarding also helps you get clear on what you want to have, be or do. And because we think in pictures, not the actual alphabetic letters, creating a visual with images that include your Big-Picture - also called your Why Factor is powerful. Allow me to explain the Why Factor for a moment.

On those days when you'd rather watch TV, or endlessly surf Facebook instead of working on your vision, your *Why* is what inspires you to action.

The Why Factor is when you aspire to achieve something that benefits other people besides you. In the grand scheme of things this perspective helps you stay focused long-term and design a life that aligns with your purpose and passion.

As previously mentioned, we all want to feel that our being on earth mattered. That we made a difference in someone's life. Because after a while, manifesting another car, house, boat, or rare-breed horse for yourself alone is plain vanity. We're happy for a season, but when the temporary emotions wear off, we may feel strangely empty inside.

That's because we're *human beings*, not *human doings*. Material things alone won't make us fulfilled. Neither does achieving more in life. Nothing wrong with both, but you and I know lots of people who have more than enough to *live on*, but nothing to *live for*.

Such people often lack big-picture dreams. They don't have a purpose-led vision. So they keep chasing possessions, power, and prestige, hoping the next thing will satisfy that aching emptiness. Many destroy themselves with work, all kinds of addictions like sex, pornography, shopping, substance abuse, or toxic relationships.

Not judging anyone here because I've been there and done that. Worked in a high-end fashion store, but came home to the bottle, questioning the sheer vanity of toiling just to buy designer labels. Like many, I got a burn-out hustling two jobs while building a side business that seemed to be thriving, but it wasn't aligned with my purpose. I worked hard to support a flashy lifestyle, but I was unhappy and disoriented in a foreign country.

Sometimes we can externally appear to have it all, but be paupers internally. As the Bible says in Mark 8:36-37, *"For what will it profit a man if he gains the whole world, and loses his own soul? Or what will a man give in exchange for his soul?"*

I'm not sharing my experiences to bash ambition, flashy lifestyles, or designer labels because I still embrace them. My point is we can have material riches *and* also enjoy a life of purpose that goes beyond this earthly experience. Again it's not an either/or question; you can be both spiritual and wealthy.

Knowing God and living out His purpose is where real success and fulfillment begins. From that state, we enjoy wealth and riches knowing our sense of worth and significance is in God, not stuff.

As we pursue our big dreams with a sense of divine purpose. We don't need to prove anything, and we're not in competition with anyone. We're complete in Jesus enjoying a state of inner peace and happiness that has no price tag.

One of the self-awareness questions I ask my coaching clients is why they want to achieve a particular goal. Once the logical *What* and the emotional *Why* are clear, they became unstoppable. So I'm now asking you the same question, why do they want to manifest a particular dream or vision?

See your Why is part of your big picture and it always involves someone else besides you. God created you with a higher purpose than climbing the corporate ladder and working to pay off your debt. There's more to life than becoming a slave to consumerism, or living in a 14-bedroomed house just to impress the neighbors, or outshine your siblings.

Again, nothing wrong corporate ladders, mortgages, and consumerism. I enjoy a good shopping spree as much as the next person. And just like any earthly Father wants good things for his children, God wants us to have and enjoy wealth. But if our sense of worth and significance comes only from possessions, power, and prestige, that my friend, is a shaky foundation to build on.

As it is written, *"Charge them that are rich in this present age, that they be not haughty, nor trust in uncertain riches, but in the living God, who gives us richly all things to enjoy."* (Timothy 6:17)

It is God who gives us the power to get wealth, and we can strive for prosperity while committing our lives and dreams to Him. As we walk with Him, our paths grow brighter, and the Why also gets clearer. He helps us grow into that purpose - both spiritually and ability-wise. We'll talk more about your Why Factor in chapter 3.

For now here's a summary of ways a faith-based vision board will support for you:

- Help you get clear on what you want to have, be, or do - so you pray specific prayers.

- Remind you of God's eternal Big-Picture - so that you keep priorities right.

- Inspire both your analytical and creative side - so you enjoy work and tedious tasks.

- Motivate you internally – so you can break down your dreams into achievable goals.

- Act as a catalyst - so that you go from dreaming to doing with action steps.

- Accelerate your results– so you get more done.

- Help you stay focused long-term - so that you don't quit in the face of obstacles.

- Help you live by design and not by default - so that you enjoy a fulfilling life of purpose and passion.

To wrap up why vision boarding works, I'd like for you to remember that we think in pictures, and as the saying goes, a picture is worth a thousand words. Vision boarding helps you externally manifest the images you conceive internally.

In the next chapter, you'll discover what exactly a vision board is and the essentials of an effective one. But first, why not take a moment to implement what we've just covered?

Workbook Actionable

Write down WHAT you want and WHY.

CHAPTER 2

WHAT A VISION BOARD IS AND THE ESSENTIALS OF AN EFFECTIVE ONE

"The one thing that you have that nobody else has is you. Your voice, your mind, your story, your vision. So write and draw and build and play and dance and live as only you can." - Neil Gaiman

Wikipedia describes a vision or dream board as *a collage of images, pictures, and affirmations of one's dreams and desires, designed to serve as a source of inspiration and motivation.*

A basic definition is; *a collection of images, words, symbols or physical trinkets that mean something to you because they represent your dreams and desires.*

Ideally, your collage serves to inspire feelings of happiness, hope, and motivation. The board is in and of itself *not* the source of these feelings, but rather a physical visual of your ideal dream life.

Vision boards vary in size and can be in physical and digital; we'll address choosing your format in chapter 7. First, let's look at some content you can put on yours.

Images. The most common item found on many vision boards. These can be photos, graphics, illustrations, paintings, drawings, mind maps, sketches or anything else that has meaning for you.

For example, if writing a book is one of your dreams, you might include a mock-up photo of your future best-seller. If your big-picture vision is to start a non-profit organization, you could have a picture representing your NGO board members. (Because it does take a team to build a dream.) If one of your desires is to go on a cruise, you could have a picture of you sunbathing on the trip you envision.

Inspiring Words. These come from different places, and for many people (me included), the primary source of inspiration is the Bible. For others, words of empowerment come from parents, role models, industry leaders, or historical figures like Mother Theresa, Mahatma Gandhi, or Martin Luther King. Maybe encouragement comes to you from a poem, a song or words from a Hallmark card. You have the freedom to choose what uplifts you.

Inspiration can also be in the form of power words that mean something to you. Words that describe who you want to become as you activate your dreams. Words like - *patient, confident, focused, or generous* are some examples. Whatever inspires you goes.

Motivational Quotes. If you're on any social media platform, you probably enjoy an occasional post like, *She Believed She Could, So She Did. Dreamers are Doers.* Or, *I Am Enough.* Such messages also found on mugs, bumper stickers, posters, and t-shirts can be extremely powerful. Because on those days when you encounter a setback and feel like quitting, a simple phrase can be enough to get you back on track.

Your board can include phrases you read or come up with, testimonials from your clients, or kind things others have said about you. Other messages can be verses or God's personal Rhema word to you.

One of the ways I use quotes is to add a short handwritten or typed version of my vision statement based on the biblical promise related to the desire. In chapter 4 we'll talk about the significance of writing down your vision statement.

Physical Objects. It can be anything that symbolizes or represents your dreams. A mock business card of your dream company. A cheque or €500 bills representing your financial freedom. The name tag of your baby reminding you of the joys of motherhood and your commitment to be a good mum.

The postcard from your relatives in Zanzibar, where you want to take a holiday. The 3-star emblem of the Mercedes-Benz you'd like to own. Your weddings invitation card, reminding you marriage starts after the beautiful wedding day.

You get the idea. Vision boards can include anything that inspires or motivates you. You're allowed to get as creative as you like because it's your vision board. So put whatever feels right for you. There are no rules, and you're not obliged to explain anything to anyone.

Besides the above content, if you want to create a compelling vision board that works for you, there are three important aspects to consider.

1. Less is more

Some vision boards have so much going on; it's overwhelming to look at them. Based on the size of your visual, sometimes less is more. Instead of an overly cluttered board that stirs up internal confusion, designing one that's not too busy can work better.

The *less is more* aspect helps you stay focused instead of spreading yourself too thin - which leads to mediocre results. As you work on your dreams, you can remove images of what you achieve and archive them in a testimonial or gratitude folder.

Because we tend to forget achievements and answered prayers quickly, this file can serve as a reminder of God's faithfulness, encouraging you on days when some dreams take longer than you'd like - which is often. Occasionally reviewing and reflecting on your past achievements and how much you've grown creates self-awareness, boosts confidence, and fans up your faith flames on those days when challenges make you second-guess your brilliance and abilities.

Only you can determine what feels overwhelming. Remember your vision board is not set in stone, you can tweak and change things as often as you like to see what works best for you. As long as it's not daily or weekly because that's akin to frequently changing the pot and soil of a new plant. Do that too often, and the roots will not go deep. The tender plant can even die due to the damage from constant digging up. So just like a plant, once you create your board, give it some time to take root instead of continually moving things around.

2. Motion

When it comes to your finished board, ideally you want images that depict people doing the dream you're activating. An effective vision board is not static. Like a piece of art that tells a story, your visual will work best with elements representing action. For example, if you want to run a marathon, you could have athletes running, or you wearing a mock-up medal. If your dream is to be a published author, you could have a photo of you holding your future book. Even better, add a photo-shopped picture of you doing a book signing with ques of people waiting. Want to become a speaker? Include an image of you speaking in front of a mock audience.

Other in-motion ideas can be you sitting in or driving your dream car. Happy children playing in the country you want to take a missions trip to. You and your partner having fun. A photo of you working out at the gym. The idea is to have photos with activity as opposed to passive looking stand-alone images. Your vision board is like a storyboard in motion with pictures and words that speak of your bright future.

3. Are you in it?

A significant essential often overlooked when vision boarding is a beautiful smiling photo. I see it often; people have lovely visuals with everyone clse on them but no personal picture of themselves.

Putting a happy picture of yourself on the vision board is a way of owning your dreams based on what you believe is possible for you. You need to externally see you in the vision because the intention is to have a physical visual that represents what you desire or already see internally with your eyes of faith.

For example, on my board is an on-going fitness and health vision. It is anchored by a beautiful picture of an active, slimmer, younger version of me. Now granted I may never go back to 60 kilos and a size 12, that picture still inspires my fitness goals. That's because the long-term goal is to be fit and have energy, irrespective of the dress size or what the scale says.

To summarize the essentials of an effective vision board, an element worth mentioning is spirituality. In the next chapter, we look at the differences between secular vision boards and faith-based ones, as well as the most crucial aspect of your dream – the source.

Before we move on, this is a good time to put down some ideas for your vision board creation.

Workbook Actionable

Write down some elements you'd like to put on your board.

CHAPTER 3

THE DIFFERENCE BETWEEN FAITH-BASED AND SECULAR VISION BOARDS

"Then the LORD answered me and said: "Write the vision and make it plain." - Habakkuk 2:2

The two significant differences between faith-based and secular vision boarding are;

1. The source of your dream.

2. The underlying motive to have, be or do something.

Let's address the source, then motive later.

Based on studying Scripture, research, and experience, I believe vision starts with God. In Bible Training, we had a class called hermeneutics, and one of the Bible study principles they taught us was that scripture interprets scripture. To get the context of what is being said in a verse, look at the chapter or passages before and after. Cross-referencing the verse in question helps to get a broader picture. This avoids building an entire doctrine based on one single verse.

The reason it's important to rightly divide the word is so that we are not tossed to and fro by strange doctrines. Not understanding the nature of God and

His word can mean the difference between dead religious activities, and a personal living relationship with our loving Creator. Allow me to briefly go off-topic and share how I went from depression, alcoholism and substance abuse to attending Bible school for two years because that testimony contributed to this book.

Although I grew up in a Christian home with a saved mother, at around 14 years, I started asking questions. The suffering and injustice I saw around me didn't seem right, so I ignorantly decided there couldn't be a God who allowed so much pain. I turned away from the Christian faith and went looking for answers.

I traveled up all kinds of roads that led to dead ends. Roads like New Age and Buddhism. I dabbled in the occult, and as an atheist used to bully, mock and harass Christians. Good thing God forgives our rebellion and ignorance because it was His love and grace that opened my eyes, leading to a come-to-Jesus prodigal daughter moment.

It was in the midst of a major life crisis that I remembered the Jesus mother introduced me to. She often told me she loved me, then added Jesus loved me more. I figured if He loved me, why not ask Him to help me - if He existed? And did He prove His love and existence! Am eternally thankful that Jesus radically transformed my whole life. Instead of the distant God that Mother and the Sunday school teachers talked about, He became my Heavenly Father. A God I now had a relationship with based on a personal experience.

For a few years, I called Jesus my Savior but didn't understand what it meant for Him to also be Lord over all the areas of my life. I still had one foot in the world and no church family. Restless, I traveled to Canada with the intention of settling there. But after a life-changing encounter, I knew Toronto had been a stop-over, not a destination. Freshly baptized and armed with a church address recommendation, I returned to Europe committed to following Jesus wholeheartedly.

Being a hungry baby Christian, I wanted to know what He had to say about everything. By nature, I like to know the *how* and *why* behind the *what*. God wired me that way for a reason. I was excited about getting "saved," and the rekindled relationship, but just like back when I was 14 years old, I had questions again.

A whole lot of questions.

Well-meaning believers and church mothers began bombarding me with answers. Most of them were about what I couldn't and shouldn't do as a Christian woman. They would show me verses like *a woman shouldn't wear pearls, gold, expensive clothing or braid her hair.* Being a black woman, the hair one was tricky. We almost come out of the womb in braids.

In addition to covering or wearing my hair in a bun, no makeup was supposed to be a sign that I was a modest, sanctified Christian woman. One sweet older church mother even showed me an old testament verse about women not wearing trousers; then she recommended I cut mine all up and make them into long skirts. Imagine that?!

At first, I was like, *OK, God, she showed me the verse and if that's what you say. I guess that's what I need to do.* But remember I like to question things, not out of arrogance, but out of curiosity and the hunger for knowledge. Before I believe in or do something, I want to have some supporting data. So I didn't cut up my trousers because some things just didn't add up. I also kept my makeup, pearls, and braids. And the church mothers and sister cliques kept their distance.

But soon the rules and regulations increased. Instead of the joy and freedom, I'd initially experienced following the "come to Jesus moment"; I began feeling burdened and rejected. Even worse, there was a tinge of resentment developing towards God. I was doing my own critical thinking, and the Church family frowned upon my questions.

I vividly remember asking God what was wrong with me wearing trouser. (Yes, we can talk to God like to a real person). I told Him I could see how some provocative and revealing dressing could cause a man struggling with lust and pornography to stumble. I understood when we love others; we want to help them overcome their temptations, not entice them. And because as believers, we are our brother's keepers, dressing scantily was not for me.

But how would my modest trousers make some men struggle with their sexuality? That seemed one-sided. As if everything was the woman's fault and responsibility. Why did this remind me of the Muslim burka? And what was the deal with not being allowed to sing in the choir because I wore pearls and gold? As my whys increased, I began wondering if I could hack these born-again religious rules.

In conversions with God, I told Him I want to obey Him out of love and reverence, but instead of His initial acceptance, I was beginning to feel like I was not good enough. The conviction that had led me to willingly want to change and turn from my former ways now felt like condemnation in His presence.

There's a huge difference between the conviction of the Holy Spirit and condemnation. The former is also called Godly sorrow, which is what leads us to repentance. (Romans 2:4) While the latter continually points out how badly we've messed up. Conviction says *come to me; I accept you* - inviting us to draw near, receive forgiveness and let God help us to change. Condemnation says *you're not good enough; you're a failure* – making us want to run and hide or rebel.

But Jesus did not come to condemn the world.

John 3:17 says *"For God did not send His Son into the world that He might condemn the world, but that the world might be saved through Him."* In Jesus we find acceptance, now that doesn't mean He approves of everything we do. No, God loves the sinner but hates the sin that separates us from Him. *"For God so loved the world that he gave his one and only Son, that whoever believes in him shall not perish but have eternal life."* (John 3:16).

You dear reader are loved by God just as you are.

On the days I went to church wearing trousers, I sensed the displeasure and distance of my pastor and church mothers. As a baby Christian, I began to feel like I had to earn God's love and my new church family's acceptance with exterior "holy" attire. To make matters worse, without realizing it, I was developing a legalistic spirit and began inwardly judging people based on their appearance. I was forgetting it was God's mercy and grace that had radically transformed me inside-out. Not my works, long skirts, or unbraided hair in a bun.

I'll spare you further boring details, but in short - I asked God to help me understand why some things were in the Bible. I wanted to know exactly what I had signed up for as a follower of Jesus. Maybe some answers would help me do the right things with the right attitude, instead of the familiar rebelliousness that was threatening to take root in my heart again.

God knows our motives and thoughts from afar, and He loves us anyway. And though He is sovereign, He doesn't want robots, so He gives us a free will. And because He also sees our hearts and struggles, if we ask, He helps us make tough decisions. It's OK to ask God to help you understand the do's and don'ts of His word.

We will not always get answers, but we can trust that His motives are pure and He always has our best interest at heart. Sometimes He explains the *why* behind the *what*, like in the garden of Eden. He not only told Adam and Eve not to eat the fruit, but He also told them why not. If they ate the forbidden fruit, they would die, both physically and spiritually - regarding their relationship with their Creator.

When God asks us not to do something, it's not because He's a ruthless dictator. It's because like a wise, protective and loving Father, He knows way more than we His children do.

God's commandments are not to take all the fun out of life on earth, but they are for our protection and eternal good. Irrespective of whether we choose to obey or not, what awes me about His nature is how He still loves us unconditionally.

This personal experience is just to show that when we commit to walk with God, He helps us. When I asked Him to help me understand His word, He led me to take steps of faith, move across the country and go to Bible school. I thought I was just going to get some theological answers and better understand His word. Little did I know God had a bigger, better plan.

He used the legalistic rules of the well-meaning don't-wear-trousers-church, and my critical thinking personality trait to lead me to His purpose. Who would have known many years down the road, I would be sharing some of what I learned in Bible school with you in a book about vision boarding?

You're not reading this book by coincidence. And if you allow Him, God will also lead and guide you into His unique plan for your life. A purpose-led vision begins with having a personal relationship with Him through Jesus. If you've never made that decision, at the end of this book, there's a short prayer and my contacts. I'd be thrilled to send you some free resources to get you started on the greatest adventure ever.

Jesus is the way to a relationship with your loving Creator, the Giver of vision and Maker of Heaven and earth. He longs to restore that friendship that was broken in the garden when Adam disobeyed God and plunged humanity into sin. The faith walk includes obeying and trusting that God loves and cares about you and all His ways are perfect.

Jeremiah 29:11 says *"He has a plan for you, to give you a hope and future."* When He is your Lord and the source of your vision, He will work all things for good, because you are called according to His purpose. Faith-based vision-boarding begins with our Creator. Let's look at how that works.

The Source

We find the favorite verse Christians use when casting vision in Habakkuk 2:2; *"Write down the vision and make it plain."* But there's a critical part often overlooked.

Remember earlier we saw the significance of cross-referencing and reading prior and after verses and chapters to get the full context? Well, if we start reading chapter 1 of Habakkuk, we see the prophet begins lamenting about the violence and evil that surrounds him. As he ponders the state of his nation and the perverted justice, he pens his questions,

"God where are you and why don't You do something?"

This is the beginning of a dialogue with God that continues into chapter 2. As Habakkuk asks questions, he also waits and listens to see what the Lord will say. And God responds, telling the author to write or record what he is seeing and hearing because the revelation will take time to unfold.

Prayer, in essence, is a dialogue. Yet we often bombard heaven with our monologues and requests, quickly say amen and get up without taking a moment to wait and hear what God has to say. Then we wonder why we don't see more prayer answers.

How often do we conclude God didn't answer a prayer, when the truth was, we didn't ask, didn't listen, didn't recognize His gentle leading, or we didn't do what He led us to do. Too often we claim to be waiting on God, while He's waiting for us.

In step 1 of the chapter on creating your vision board, we get practical on how to get the dream by actively listening. For now, let's look at some Bible study techniques to see how Habakkuk's passage applies to vision-boarding.

Besides the *scripture interprets scripture* rule of thumb, there's another interpretation technique called *primary and secondary application.* Primary application means considering what the scripture meant to the person or people it was initially written to. For example, was it written to the Jews in the old testament, messianic believers in the new testament, newly converted Gentiles, or the (church) body of Christ today?

Secondary application means looking at how the principles in a passage can apply to you and me in a practical way today. Just as the primary application of the Ten Commandments was to the Jews in the old testament, the secondary application still applies today.

By the same token, the primary application in the Habakkuk passage is addressing prophecy about the end times. By applying the secondary application, we can take these timeless truths in Habakkuk chapter 2:1-2 and apply them to our individual lives today. As 2 Timothy 3:16-17 states; *"All Scripture is God-breathed and is useful for teaching, rebuking, correcting and training in righteousness, so that the servant of God may be thoroughly equipped for every good work."*

A lot of Christians get nervous when they hear vision boards because we don't want to dabble in the secular law of attraction and New Age practices. But remember Satan is an imitator who never has and never will create anything. He takes what's pure and twists it, leaving God out and perverting spiritual principles.

Is a vision board an ungodly practice? A short Bible study yields some answers, further clarifying the difference between faith-based and secular vision boarding. Get your bible if you wish, and together, let's take a very close look at the original Hebrew meaning of the verse. I recommend the study tools on eSword.com or a concordance if you want to dig deeper.

Habakkuk asks questions, and when he listens, God answers and instructs him to *"Write the vision and make it plain on tablets, That he may run who reads it."* (Habakkuk 2:2) Let's interpret this English verse below word for word (**in bold**) using the original Hebrew language it was written in.

In the Strong's Bible dictionary, the words are:

Write - *Kâthab*; in Hebrew means: to *write* (describe, inscribe, prescribe, subscribe, record).

Vision -*Chazown;* in Hebrew means: *from a sight (mentally)*, i.e., a dream, (in the night or of the heart), revelation, or oracle.

Make it Plain – *Bâ'ar*; in Hebrew means: *make it plain* means to *dig*; by analogy to *engrave*; figuratively to *explain:* - declare, (make) plain (-ly).

Tablets – *Lûach lûach;* in Hebrew means: a *tablet* (as *polished*), of stone, wood or metal: - board, plate, table.

That – *Ma'an;* the Hebrew meaning: *in order that:* - because of, to the end (intent).

Run – *Rûts;* Hebrew meaning: *especially to rush:* - break down, divide speedily, footman, guard, bring hastily, (make) run (away, through), post, stretch out.

Reads - *Qârâ' kaw-raw';* the Hebrew meaning:

(identical to the idea of accosting a person met). *To call out to* (that is, properly address by name, but used in a wide variety of applications): - call (for, forth, self, upon), (make) proclaim (-ation), pronounce, publish, say.

Did you see that? Here's the summary of the Hebrew translation:

"Record, describe, a sight (mental, a dream or revelation of the heart) on a board or tablet"!

Why?

"So that the reader hasten and makes rapid progress with what she proclaims or publishes"!

I don't know about you, but if we ponder on the above, it looks like what the New Age secular world teaches about vision boards is based on the biblical principle from Habakkuk. The difference is a lot of things are twisted. The glaring one; focus on what you want and leave God out of the picture.

By the way, Buddha, Allah, Source, and Universe are not the same as the Christian God. The God of the Bible laid down His majesty and became a man, born of the Virgin Mary. It all started in the Garden of Eden when Adam and Eve chose to believe the serpent's (devil) lies and did what God asked them not to do; eat from the tree of the knowledge of good and evil.

Their disobedience broke their fellowship with God, and consequently, every human being after that was by default born into a fallen world with a sin-nature. Until God became Jesus Christ. The only person without sin who qualified to pay the price of redeeming fallen man. He was crucified and died to take our place bearing the judgment that was ours.

But just as foretold thousands of years in the Bible,

He didn't stay in the grave but broke the power of sin and death when and rose again. He did this out of love for you and me. To reconcile us back to Himself.

That, in essence, is the gospel. All it takes to restore the broken fellowship with the living God is believing the good news of Jesus Christ, repenting of a sinful life and inviting Him into your heart. We don't have to first be "good" people, neither do we have to worry about hacking the saved life and being perfect Christians.

It's an internal, supernatural transformation where God helps us day by day. Years later I'm still a work in progress, clay in my Potters hands. Saved by grace, walking by faith in the One who begins and completes the good work in us. If you're not sure how to invite Jesus to be your Lord, the prayer at the end of this book will guide you.

OK, now that we've clarified which God we're talking about here, remember if you believe otherwise, am not judging you. I can relate because I've been where you are - seeking answers to life's tough questions. God gave us a free will because He loves us with the agape love that allows freedom of choice. We can seek answers and choose what we want to believe. We can accept the good news or reject it.

If you're a seeker, know that the God of the Bible loves you unconditionally and He sees your heart and desires. If you ask Him to reveal Himself to you, He will. But don't take my word for it, a personal experience beats an opinion in a book any day.

Bank tellers don't learn to spot counterfeit money by studying the counterfeits. They study genuine bills until they master the look of the real thing. Then when they see the bogus money, they recognize it. We reviewed Habakkuk's vision-casting, now let's briefly look at how New Agers do vision boards.

They say focus on what you want, look at your vision board daily, you'll attract the stuff you see on it and "source" or "the universe" is who you give credit to. But the Bible exhorts us first to ask, (pray), listen to what God says, then record what we receive in our hearts. By faith, we believe and see the vision internally before seeing it physically.

The physical visual is so we can run with it (action) and we call it forth (affirmations) because it may take time to manifest. Hebrews 11:1 says *"Faith is the evidence of things not seen, the substance of things hoped for."* So after you believe in your heart that what God said to you is possible, you now have hope of those things right? A vision board then can serve as the evidence of things not yet seen (with the physical eye). It helps you stay focused, as you run and take action towards turning the invisible dream into tangible substance.

In Genesis when God promised Abraham, a son, He (God) took him outside and told him to look up to the skies and count the stars. That's how many sons he (Abraham) would have. He fell asleep counting the stars, looking at a physical representation of what he believed and received in his spirit as God promised.

This chapter is not meant to coerce you into anything you don't feel comfortable doing. As mentioned this book is based on experiences and opinions I put together as a result of research, prayer and the transformation my clients and I have gotten. What works for us may not work for you, and that's fine. We're individually led by the Holy Spirit, with the written word as the foundation. After the source of vision, let's address motives.

The Motive

The second defining difference between faith-based and secular vision boards is the motive behind the desire. Let's say your dream is something material - a nice car, a big house or a holiday cruise. All very valid needs that don't require deep theological reasons before taking action. We don't have to over-spiritualize the desire for the material things we want and ask for. But it's good to check our hearts and see if our motives need adjusting.

The Amplified version of James 4:3 says, *"You ask [God for something] and do not receive it, because you ask with wrong motives [out of selfishness or with an unrighteous agenda], so that [when you get what you want] you may spend it on your [hedonistic] desires."*

Sometimes we don't even know the motive behind why we do or want something. But if we allow God to search our hearts, He'll reveal hidden agendas, then help us adjust what's off.

As mentioned earlier, if your reason to have, be, or do something is to keep up with the Joneses, or outshine your siblings, that's a shaky foundation. By the same token, if you believe your happiness and contentment hinges solely on acquiring a new BMW and that bigger house, you're setting yourself up for disappointment. If the motive behind achieving a particular dream or vision is to have a sense of importance before men, that my friend will leave you disillusioned.

Your value and worth are not based on your accomplishments or lack thereof. God loves you simply because you are. His is not performance-based acceptance. You are enough just as you are. We don't have to earn His love or impress Him with our achievements.

Previously we saw that it's possible to have wealth and serve God at the same time. It's not an either/or situation. We can richly enjoy things money can buy, as long as the material things don't have priority over our Creator and people.

Because we're merely stewards of possessions on earth, we're to use things and love people. Not love things and use people. Money, wealth and riches are for meeting our needs and blessing others on earth. Not for hoarding as a source of security and significance. Lest we become like the rich fool Jesus warned us about when he said;

"Watch out! Guard yourselves against every form of greed, for a man's life does not consist in the abundance of his possessions." Then He told them a parable: "The ground of a certain rich man produced an abundance. So he thought to himself, 'What shall I do since I have nowhere to store my crops?' Then he said, 'This is what I will do: I will tear down my barns and will build bigger ones, and there I will store up all my grain and my goods. Then I will say to myself, "You have plenty of good things laid up for many years. Take it easy. Eat, drink, and be merry!"'

But God said to him, 'You fool! This very night your life will be required of you. Then who will own what you have accumulated?' This is how it will be for anyone who stores up treasure for himself but is not rich toward God."

As we wrap up the difference between faith-based and secular vision boarding, the defining point is that our focus, *expectations, and* fulfillment are not on the board, but on God. The visual in and of itself is not unbiblical, but rather a tool to work with when activating your dreams. You can also choose to only have a written vision list without all the other essentials we discussed in chapter 2.

Check your heart and let peace lead you. Because, in the next chapter, we look at six core areas you can vision board about. Remember to add some action to this chapter's inspiration in your workbook.

WORKBOOK ACTIONABLE

Take a moment and answer some soul-searching questions about the source and motives behind your dream(s).

CHAPTER 4

6 CORE AREAS THAT VISION BOARDS IMPROVE

"Don't underestimate the power of your vision to change the world. Whether that world is your office, your community, an industry or a global movement, you need to have a core belief that what you contribute can fundamentally change the paradigm or way of thinking about problems."
- Leroy Hood

When helping my coaching clients achieve their dreams and goals, we work with a popular, simple, but powerful tool called *The Wheel of Balance*. It has six core areas, and each area is essential if we're to enjoy holistic success.

If we completely ignore one or more of the six core areas, we have dis-harmony. Like trying to drive with a flat or unbalanced tire. The success journey gets bumpy, dangerous, and even life-threatening.

We can get dis-stressed, depressed and dis-eased.

We go through life feeling unfilled, which can lead to bad decisions as we try to find balance, or fill a void. Have you ever chased the wrong things or sacrificed important areas like health and relationships on the altar of your job or business? I've been there. Not wise.

Using the Wheel of Balance template creates self-awareness and helps locate any imbalances, so you can course-correct and enjoy life's journey. The recommended bonus workbook has resources for a quick self-assessment. There are theme worksheets with different core areas that you can replace or change to suit your life. For example, if your vision doesn't include a business dream, instead you can put career, as a core area. Instructions on how to do this valuable exercise are in the free masterclass video.

Wheel of Balance

Below are six core areas you can vision board on.

1. Faith and Fulfillment

"Faith gives us an inner strength and a sense of balance and perspective in life." - Zig Gregory Peckt

Purpose-led vision and balanced success starts with having our priorities right. It is written when we *seek God's kingdom first, all the other things will be added unto us.* (Mathew 6:33) When our relationship with our Creator is healthy, there is peace, joy and a sense of fulfillment.

We stop chasing the wrong things, trying to fill the God-shaped void in our hearts. One of the saddest things to see is when someone has all the material things money can buy, yet they have such an aching sense of emptiness that they question the very essence of this beautiful gift we call life.

Having priorities right allows you to enjoy the rewards of your labor, with gratitude to the One who gives us the power to get wealth. A simple, but powerful verse on your vision board can serve as a reminder of the things that will matter into eternity. Because when our earthly journey ends and the casket is shut, no one takes any material stuff with them.

2. Fitness and Health

"It is health that is real wealth and not pieces of gold and silver." - Mahatma Gandhi

The impact physical and mental well-being has on success is often underestimated. Fact is when you're physically fit; it's much easier to stay motivated as you take action steps towards your dreams.

The lifestyle choices we make affect our health, both positively or negatively. For example, did you know that exercising is hugely beneficial to your mental health? Studies reveal that the `feel good´ hormones released during exercises like cycling, swimming or running can also relieve the symptoms of depression.

As you're working on your vision and goals, there will be days where you feel overwhelmed, if you can't go to the gym, at least take a walk. Exercising is a great way to clear your mind, get energized, and stay focused. Despite knowing these benefits, like many people, I too struggle with my fitness goals and have to get creative to be consistent.

Let's talk about health for a moment, how's yours doing? For many in the corporate world and online entrepreneurs, it could be better. Many of us have a sedentary lifestyle. We spend lots of time indoors hunched over our computers. We don't drink enough water, often eat at our desks, and hardly exercise.

Vision-boarding can help and here's how; having a visual that includes healthy lifestyle intentions will prompt you to take steps to stay fit. Our bodies experience wear and tear, and if you neglect yours consistently and ignore the core area of health, one of two things will happen. Either you'll have to spend your hard-earned money on doctors and medications, or lifestyle diseases like diabetes, high blood pressure, or some stress-related illness will snatch your life away before your time.

Studies prove exercise, healthy eating, adequate sleep, and drinking enough water can prevent some sickness and even avert an early death. You need a healthy body and mind to achieve your dreams and purpose, so take good care of yours. It's the only one you have. When it breaks down, you can't walk into a store and get a quick replacement or spare parts.

3. Family and Friends

"Cherish your human connections - your relationships with friends and family."
- Barbara Bush

Our relationships affect our health, emotions, and productivity. A toxic relationship can leave you drained - with feelings of despair and anger. Unhappiness and rage can lead to depression, which in turn can cause failure and stall progress due to bad decisions. Mental health issues related to toxic relationships can even lead to early death as studies reveal prolonged chronic stress causes cancer.

When 729 people were followed over 12 years by

the University of Rochester and Harvard School of Public Health, studies found a 70% increase in cancer deaths for the individuals whose level of suppressing emotions was above 75%.

A report by the Journal of Psychosomatic Research reveals that according to a study conducted by the King's College Hospital in London, after a detailed psychological interview and a self-administered questionnaire, the most commonly identified characteristic of 160 breast cancer patients was extreme suppression of anger.

Toxic relationships are deadly, but healthy ones can add years to your life and accelerate your success. When you have inner and outer peace, you have the emotional, mental and physical capacity to make better decisions. The support you get from loved ones on tough days eases stress and makes celebrating milestones together fun.

We often don't have any family or friendship goals, but vision boarding helps bring clarity on how to nurture healthy relationships that boost longevity. Some question to help you get started with your relationship dreams can be:

- What kind of relationships would help you function better?

- What kind of person do you have to became to qualify for those relationships?

- How can you be a better partner, friend, brother, sister, son, daughter, boss, colleague?

- How do you and your partner want to feel about your marriage five years from now?

- How can you best support your children?

Examine your relationships, and see how they are impacting your life. If you need to reassess some connections, (even toxic family members) take them to God in prayer and ask Him for help and wisdom.

Iron sharpens iron and we could all benefit from relationships that bring out the best in us. Not lead us to an early grave because we suppressed negative emotions that caused cancer.

So put visuals on your vision board that represents the kind of relationships you desire, then turn around and begin to be the kind of person you want to attract or have around you. Sow good relationship seeds because, in life, we reap what we sow and attract what we believe we deserve.

4. Finances and Business

"Money isn't the most important thing in life, but it's reasonably close to oxygen on the "gotta have it" scale." – Zig Ziglar

This is one of the most popular themes on vision boards. Many of us have goals when it comes to money, business and wealth. Which is normal because we all need the legal tender to operate on planet earth.

There's nothing wrong with wanting to be wealthy, and contrary to a misquoted verse, money is not the root of all evil. It's the love of it that is the root of all evil. But did you know one doesn't have to be wealthy to love money? It's possible to have none at all but still, love it. Poor and rich people can love money.

One of the reasons many people don't reach their financial goals is because of mental blocks and limiting beliefs about money and wealth.

We entertain a scarcity mindset and negative thoughts like:

- You can't afford that.
- If others make more, you'll make less.
- More money means you pay more taxes.
- You are not qualified enough to earn that much money.
- Having wealth is not safe because people hate rich folks.
- What if you make some then lose it? You'll look like a failure.
- You've never been good with numbers or, you're financially illiterate.
- If you get rich, your current friends or family may envy or resent you.

When we knowingly or unknowingly allow these voices to take root in our hearts, we believe them and look for evidence to prove ourselves right. In essence, we sabotage ourselves.

And unless we take steps to renew our minds and silence those lies, we'll never see the manifestation of the abundance God has promised us in this life. But an inspiring, purpose-based vision board can help here as well.

Examples of some self-awareness questions you can ask yourself are:

- What does money mean to me?
- What does my version of financial freedom look like?
- When all my needs are met, and I have extra

income left over, what will my *money with a mission* factor be?

- How can I change my part of the world?
- Who would I love to help if money and time were not an issue?

While answering these questions, look up promises that inspire possibility thinking and an abundance mindset. As you start to envision yourself having more than enough to bless others, get images that represent the needs you'll meet with the increase that's coming.

How about a bigger house where you can host guests? A beach home where you can relax and hold retreats. Maybe you dream of starting a youth center, donating to a soup kitchen, giving to your favorite charity or missionary. Helping a struggling friend.

If your vision is business-related, think about questions like:

- What is your definition of a successful business you'll enjoy building?
- What kind of ideal client pays you to solve their problems?
- How many clients or how much revenue would you like in an ideal year?
- Imagine the future business owner you are, what does your typical day look like?

Include visuals on your board that represent your dream business, your ideal clients and desired income as you reflectively answer these questions. We have a big God, so allow yourself to dream big. Cast down the limiting beliefs and expand your vision because *"God is able to do exceedingly, abundantly above and beyond all we can ask or think."* (Ephesians 3:20)

5. Fun and Self-Care

"People who cannot find time for recreation are obliged sooner or later to find time for illness."
- John Wanamaker

All work and no play makes Jack a dull boy, cliche but true. Recreation plays a significant role in your success. And while goofing around when you could be working on your goals is not smart, downtime will boost your productivity. As you work on your dreams, know that slowing down to laugh, play and smell the roses is not a waste of time. Nurturing your soul and emotions will keep you in the game long-term.

A life without wellness and self-care can lead to burning the candle at both ends. When this happens, you have a hard time staying focused. Your vision is no longer fun, and if you keep pushing too hard, you risk burning out. I learned this lesson the hard way. Always being on hustle, push and grind mode is not wisdom. And *"I'm SO busy"* is not a badge of honor.

If you're an ambitious high-achieving go-getter, self-care and wellness is not a luxury, but a priority. Downtime can be as simple as getting a massage, watching a play, or gardening. Creative activities like painting, playing an instrument, or coloring in books. Maybe as a guy, you unwind by playing chess, video games or golf. The idea is to unwind and get lost in something that takes your mind off work.

Besides Pilates, Spa-days, girls nights and Netflix, I enjoy shoe-shopping, Zumba, and Filofax decorating. Being an introvert, time spent alone reading is like a mini-holiday that takes care of my mindset. Karaoke or singing in a Gospel choir takes care of the soul connections.

Your vision board can include images that represent fun, wellness, rest, and rejuvenation. Maybe cook-outs relax you. Have a picture of you and your loved ones enjoying a meal. Does a day at the spa recharge your batteries? Have a related visual. Does sport equal wellness for you? Have an image with you or someone performing the sports activity. Whatever recreation means to you, include something inspiring on your dream board without overthinking.

6. Future and Legacy

"That is your legacy on this Earth when you leave this Earth: how many hearts you touched."
- Patti Davis

If so far your vision board has only been about you; this is where you can add something purpose-related. Remember it's about activating your dreams, and you're allowed to dream big.

Imagine if all the desires in the above core areas manifested, and time and money were not an issue, what would you look forward to doing tomorrow? What would your ideal future - 1, 5, 10, or even 20 years from now look like? What dream will speak about you long after you're gone?

For some ideas, think Nelson Mandela, Martin Luther King, Mother Theresa and other inspiring people whose legacy continues to impact us, years after they checked out of planet earth. Your inspiration doesn't have to come from famous people; it could be someone no one knows about but you. A person who left a positive impact on your life.

You can include an element that reminds you of the Big-Picture. Something that will positively affect other people, whether you live to see the vision fulfilled or not. Take a moment and allow yourself to shatter the glass ceiling in your mind, dare to imagine the kind of legacy you desire to leave. What would that be for you? If you could wave a magic wand, what would you like to change for the sole benefit of others?

Including visuals about your legacy on your vision board, is not so you overthink things, feel intimidated and get all stressed out. Instead, let it serve as a fun, pressure-free anchor for your long-term dreams. A visual that represents God's purpose for your life and reminds you that dreaming is a beautiful thing. Because who knows, your legacy dreams may manifest in your lifetime!

So go ahead and dare to follow your heart on this one too, because in the next chapter I show you how to create your compelling vision board. But before you turn the page, take a moment and internalize what we've covered in this chapter.

Do you have balance in life?

How are your six core areas doing?

Workbook Actionable
Do the Wheel of Balance self-assessment.

CHAPTER 5

7 -STEP GUIDE TO CREATING YOUR VISION BOARD

"Delight yourself also in the Lord, And He shall give you the desires of your heart." - Psalm 37:4

1. Dream

Faith-based vision-boarding begins by conceiving the dream internally. Earlier we saw vision originates from God and it can come in different ways. Like when He speaks to us through His written word, we associate with someone who is doing what we feel led to do, or it just seems right to do something. Your dream can be activated after the Wheel of Balance self-assessment, a book, a defining moment, or an event.

Remember Habakkuk? Schedule time, go to a quiet spot, relax and ask God what's His will for you. Then without being in a hurry, listen with your inner ear and observe your mental screen. What do you see or hear? I don't mean an actual voice, but an impression in your spirit. If it seems like you're not getting anything, don't get frustrated, sometimes God will answer us when we're doing something else. So keep an open and expectant heart. So keep an open and expectant heart because Jesus promised that as His sheep we hear His voice. Ideally, this step is where you want to read portions of scripture or promises related to the requests and needs you have.

You can also imagine your ideal life in 1, 3, or 5 years, what do you want to have, be or do in the six core areas? Envision the end result as much as possible and allow yourself to imagine the future you living the dream.

Where are you and what are you doing?

Who's there with you?

How do you look and feel?

What sights and sounds surround you?

Do you see you fulfilling those God-given desires?

Alternatively, you might want to meditate on a particular verse or promise God gives you. You could be reading the Bible or a book, and a verse literally seems to jump out of the pages. Or an impression, a phrase, or an image comes to your mind while you're quietly communing with the Lord. Draw what your inner eye sees, or write what your inner ear hears.

Without overthinking about how on earth it could ever happen, you could also imagine it's December 31st, and you're reviewing what has been your ideal year. What does it look like? What promises has God fulfilled and how do you feel?

Psalm 37:4 promises that if we *delight in the Lord; He will give us the desires of our hearts*. But before you get hung up on the *"I'm delighting myself in the Lord and are these desires from Him?"* question, here's an easy way to move along. Invite Him to give you a vision that aligns with His Big Picture. Desires that will influence others positively and bring Him glory. Then commit your dreams to Him.

Thinking of who else will benefit is part of purpose-led vision boarding. A desire may seem fickle or vain, but if you look beyond your own benefit, you'll see the bigger picture and purpose. It doesn't have to be some grandiose, world-changing thing - a pebble in the water creates a ripple effect.

Below are some examples of big-picture thinking.

Let's say you desire to write a book; purpose - you'll serve the world with your know-how.

You want to build a successful business; purpose - solving people's problems and get paid for it.

You desire a partner; purpose – marriage is God's idea because two are better than one. We're complete in Christ, but as a couple, you'll achieve more together.

You want financial freedom; purpose - money with a mission allows us to help build God's kingdom and be a blessing to others.

See how this works?

Big-picture thinking is not complicated when we remember we're all interconnected. Somebody on earth is waiting for you to take your place and live your dream. Somebody somewhere will benefit when you achieve success.

That's what purpose-led vision-boarding is about. Thinking beyond our own needs and desires. I'll repeat - God doesn't mind us having material things, as long as those things don't have our hearts.

2. Define

Were you able to sit for a quiet moment with God and get some answers? Did you practice seeing yourself experiencing the manifested dream? If not, please don't miss this important step. It's the foundation for step two.

Focused thinking and allowing yourself to imagine and experience the vision as if it's happening is also called visualizing. Science proves that thinking about something can cause your brain to release certain chemicals that create new neural pathways in the brain. These thoughts become things!

As mentioned earlier, you might want to google Dr. Caroline Leaf's work on how scripture confirms science. Add positive, strong emotions, and the mind can not differentiate between a real event and one you visualize in your thoughts. Imagination is a very powerful thing.

So if you imagined your God-given desire as a reality, how did that feel? I confess visualizing success both exhilarates and scares me some. Because it feels so good, I get happy. I smile. I enjoy the daydreaming. And then, the more I think about it, the more I want it to be real. But I also know to ever experience those feelings manifested, I will have to get off my behind and take some action. That's exciting and scary.

This kind of reality check is vital because, after the focused thinking and feel-good emotions, it's time to open your eyes. After you think it, you have to ink it, so you get the vision out of the invisible realm of your mind out into the physical realm.

Get a pen and paper, take a few minutes and write the vision down. Define it clearly on paper and let your warm eyeballs rest on the words you write.

Here again, science confirms scripture when it comes to *"Write down the vision and make it plain."* Here's why writing it down on paper with a pen (not typing) is vital: Neuroscience reveals that a powerful connection happens between your brain and hand when you physically write things down.

Below are three reasons why you get better results and achieve your intentions faster and with ease when you write them down.

1. Clarity - Writing sorts through the mental clutter as you formulate your dreams and thoughts.

2. Memory boost - Research suggests we remember up to 90% of what we physically write down.

3. Reticular Activating System - Raises your awareness, so you recognize opportunities and see solutions related to your vision while filtering out all unrelated data.

One crucial point about writing your vision statement is to keep it positive. Instead of *I don't want to be fat*, write; *I am physically fit and weigh 75 kilos*. Instead of *I don't want to be broke*, write something like, *Because God supplies all of my needs, I have more than enough to be a blessing to others.* If you want to change something, turn it around to a positive statement of faith that feels good. I like to include a related Bible promise to the vision statement.

3. Determine

Designing a vision board can be as simple as cutting images out of a magazine and pinning them on to your cork board. Or yours can be a work of art with personal drawings, physical trinkets, and photos you shoot. Here are three board options:

Physical: Your creative possibilities are endless. Cork boards, construction paper, folders, bulletin boards, whiteboards, glass frames, or a wall in your home or office. Just bear in mind unless it's a book or folder, the portability of this board is limited.

Digital: Boards created with software like Photoshop, Canva or any image-editing tool are convenient. They're not only portable but easy to quickly edit. You can add text, and paste scanned personal photos.

Mobile: I'm yet to try these which are created on an app made for digital devices. Here you also have the advantage of having inspiration on the go. You can take your vision board everywhere you go.

Quick recap, so far you envisioned your desire manifested, released happy hormones associated with achievement. Then you defined your vision on paper, getting it out of the unseen into the seen realm, well done! You've done the initial hard work of creating your board. All that's left here is to determine your preferred format.

1. Physical - a cork board, whiteboards, framed glass picture, or a board out of construction (craft paper).

2. Book - spiral notebook or a folder.

3. Digital - designed with photo editing software or a web-based App.

A hybrid option I use is designing a framed board to hang on my workstation, then I take a photo and use that image as a screen-saver on my digital devices. Once you've settled on what works best for you, get the corresponding supplies you need.

Creating Physical Boards - Crafting supplies, ornaments, photos, postcards, pens, paper, board magnets, push pins, spiral notebook or folder, trinkets. Have magazines, scissors, and glue ready.

Creating Digital Boards – If you opt for a digital version, head on over to Pinterest or Google and find images related to your vision. Digital boards have the advantage of being less messy than physical ones and easy to recreate quickly.

I used Canva to create the example in the introduction section of this book. I show you step-by-step how to quickly create your own in the Design Your Vision Board online course. You can also Google web-based apps like Jack Canfield's Success Vision Board app to create a digital version.

4. Develop

You've settled on your format and gotten supplies; it's crafting time. Dedicate a minimum of 30 minutes for this step because it's the "meat and potatoes" of vision boarding. Get your favorite beverage; tea, coffee, smoothie, whatever you enjoy. Choose some music and let it play softly in the background. Get comfortable on the floor or sit on a table with your drink, board, book or folder and your supplies. Then start flipping through the magazines.

Without overthinking, pullout images that speak to you on impulse. You may stop at some pictures that at first glance seem unrelated to your desire. But if they seem to jump off the page and for some reason you feel happy or drawn to them, go ahead and cut them out. Sometimes our spirit knows things our mind does not yet know. Time will tell. Stay open to possibilities with the switch of faith turned on.

If your format is digital, work with Photoshop, Canva, or a web-based app. Whatever you work with today, remember you can always change the format later or have both physical and digital versions. Have the vision statement you wrote earlier on standby in case you want to paste it on your physical board or type it on your digital version. You can also cut and stick power words in beautiful typography that appeals to you.

Once you've gathered enough images, power words and your vision statement, it's time to develop the vision you have internally into a beautiful physical visual. Remember the Kodak days, before digital cameras, smartphones, and selfies? The negative film roll was developed in a dark room. We're doing something similar here, but not in a dark room. Music in the background, scented candles, faith, and happy vibes are suggested essentials as you develop your vision board. Maybe it's been a while since you played with glue and scissors, give yourself permission to have fun.

After you're done cutting out pictures, arrange your images, quotes and anything else you want on your board. Be as creative as you like. You could add crafting supplies like fabric, wool or ribbons. How about finger painting, gluing seashells or sand? Anything goes as you place your elements.

Your arrangement can be random, done according to the general themes in the bonus workbook templates. Or you can carefully set your elements according to the wheel of balance core areas. You can have different boards for each area, or be intuitive and go with the flow. It's your board, allow your creativity to flow and do what feels right for you.

The Wheel of Balance

Worksheet

(Theme Ideas)

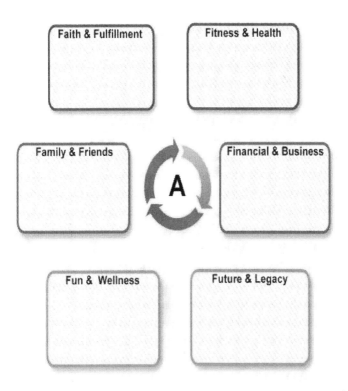

5. Describe

This step helps you use both the left and right brain thinking. It's best done immediately after you finish developing your visual. To stay in the flow, I recommend stepping back for a moment to take in what you've just created. Take a short break to stretch or look at your work of art for a few minutes.

Then sit down with pen and paper and describe your vision board. Write as if you were explaining to a blind person or someone on the other end of the telephone. What are the 1000 words you would use to describe your visual? Interpret the arranged elements into a written version of your ideal story-board.

As you physically describe your vision board on paper, your inner critic may start speaking to you. First with soft, but negative suggestions in your mind like:

What do you think you're doing here?

This is so ridiculous, and you look a joke.

What makes you imagine this dream is possible?

If you ignore the inner critic and continue writing, the voices may become loud and take on a bullying, harsher tone saying things like:

You've just wasted time on some silly childish-looking thing.

You of all people could never achieve this outrageous vision!

Remember that time you didn't achieve (XYZ), what makes you think this will be different?

Stop right now! This will be another faith-failure, and you'll look like a fool.

It's important to understand what's happening here; while the inner critic often tries to protect us from pain and hurting ourselves, it also keeps us trapped in the very zoo and comfort zone we desire to escape. If we don't question and neutralize those limiting beliefs, we sabotage ourselves. There are different types of mindset strategies to deal with the inner critic and release dis-empowering beliefs. For now, am going to share a simple one that works well for many of my coaching clients and myself.

First, silently acknowledge the inner critic. For a split second take note of what the negative fear-based voices are saying. Then revert your full attention back to your inspiring visual and notice something else - there are two voices going on here. As you look at your board, the negative chatter is going on in your mind. At the same time what you're looking at externally (your visual) is also talking to you. But positively. Do you notice the fear versus faith voices? We have a choice about who we will yield to.

Now answer the inner critic's valid or invalid concerns and accusations by speaking out the positive words you're writing to describe your board. The answering can also be reading your vision statement out loud, based on the promises God gave you earlier.

You can use a gentle, but firm voice, or a loud and passionate tone. It doesn't have to be combative, but you do need to be assertive and speak out. And here's why; it's hard to meditate on negative thoughts while speaking out loud simultaneously. Try this for a second - in your mind, silently start counting backwards from number 10 to zero. Are you counting? Good. Now stop and say your name out loud. Can you tell me what number you were on when you spoke your name out loud?

Most people can't recall. That's because speaking out loud interrupts the inner dialogues and mental chatter which is often worry, fear, doubt, and the enemy's lies. This step helps you do some mindset work so you can move on despite the inner critic's well-meaning attempts to protect you. We can choose faith over fear using the power of the spoken word. When tempted by the devil, Jesus answered and said: *"It is written."*

6. Decide

Now that you're done developing and describing your vision board, how do you feel? Are you experiencing a healthy dose of nervous energy? That's normal; it happens when you step out of your comfort zone. This kind of nervousness is positive stress that internally primes us to take the next step. Many top achievers, speakers, and athletes say they experience it every single time before they start performing.

Before every presentation, whether it's podcasting, video, consulting, coaching, doing a business training or a public talk, I always get positive stress. So don't draw back. You've made good progress and gathered momentum very nicely. Stay in the flow because after the creative fun part; this step is just as important. But first, let 's briefly look at all you've achieved.

By now you're inspired by the possibilities, and you have a beautiful visual. Your reticular activating system is ready to work for you, (but only if you physically wrote down your vision). If you didn't write it on paper, you're sabotaging your success. Stop here, go back and complete the define step. If you followed through with all the previous steps, happy brain chemicals are released when you think of, or look at your vision board. Newton's law states that an object in motion stays in motion – we want to keep moving.

Sadly this is where many visionaries drop the ball and remain stuck in the zoos of life. They skip this crucial step and wonder why they fail to achieve their intentions. Many become disillusioned and cynical. But that doesn't have to be you. Here's how not to become disillusioned despite all the fantastic work you've done - make a quality decision. Commit to doing one thing that brings you closer to manifesting your dream(s), then take that leap.

The proof that a decision has been made is in the corresponding action taken. In my *Achieve Your Goals* course, I call this - getting things done with MSM steps.

MSM stands for **M**icro. **S**mall. **M**edium. You want to first brain dump, make a plan, then schedule one micro-step to take. Sounds pretty simple, but micro steps are powerful because they keep the momentum going. Just like the law of gravity, Newton's law works, for those who work it.

See, it's one thing to have a gorgeous visual, but you also have to take daily action to achieve it. After creating your board, you want to have a plan of how you'll make the dream happen. The five simple steps in the *Achieve Your Goals* online course shows you how to accelerate your success with MSM steps.

Having a plan and a system to follow helps you stay focused and fast-track your progress. If you followed along the steps, you should have a beautiful visual that internally inspires you to take the next step.

If you need further support with the action-taking, use the recommended resources at the end of this book. You qualify for a 20% discount on the *Achieve Your Goals* online course and other digital downloads because you're reading this book. To claim your course discount, use the coupon in your free workbook.

Now to the last vision board creation step that separates dreamers from doers. It's simple but a reason many fail to achieve their dreams. You've read this far already, let's make sure you remain the action-taker you are.

7. Do It Daily

The success or failure of your vision board could be determined by this step so please pay attention (just like you've been doing all along). After the initial excitement of creating your visual wanes a bit, you can't put the board in a closet, go watch hours of TV then "hope and pray" your dreams come knocking on your door.

Yes, a vision board activates your dreams, but this doesn't mean all you do now is stare at it long and hard enough hoping to "attract" and "manifest" your success. No, you'll have to follow-up with some work.

Taking inspired action is another difference between faith-based and many law-of-attraction vision boards. Following your dreams goes beyond designing a vision board, and just like anything worth achieving, it takes consistent work. It is written, *"Faith without works is dead."* (James 2:26) So instead of the *law of attraction*, I prefer the *law of action*. Like all laws, it works if you work it.

Results will be faster and easier if you put your visual where you see it often. But more importantly here's what separates the disillusioned cynics from those who get results; every single day, or every time you catch a glimpse of your board, ask yourself, this question, "*What action step can I take today towards my dreams?*" It doesn't have to be a huge step. In fact, micro-steps or something called Kaizen will work better long-term.

Kaizen is a Japanese philosophy that focuses on continual improvement. The key is to stay in motion with sustainable small steps taken consistently. Kaizen-ing will bring you further than a huge leap that initially feels overwhelming and scary.

In a nutshell, as I show you in the Achieve Your Goals eCourse, break down your vision into projects and tasks using micro, small and medium goals. Then decide on a daily action step. Schedule it, do it and track your progress. Do this every day, and you now have a vision board in action.

But there's one thing that stops many of us from taking action. Fear. Fear of failure, fear of success, or fear of the unknown are common ones that keep us stuck in the zoos of life. One of the best ways to face and neutralize fear is to simply taking action. Start somewhere but move from theory, overthinking and planning. Do something that gives you a mini-positive outcome.

However tiny your tangible results are, they will build up your confidence fueling more action. So go on and as the slogan says – Just Do It (daily). Because even God can not steer a parked car. Dream big, then start small. Put some works to your faith and watch Him surprise you.

This concludes the 7-step guide to vision-boarding. Now that you know the law of action is a deciding factor, in the next and last chapter, we'll look at a few reasons why vision boards fail. You'll discover some things to avoid, so you don't sabotage your success.

Remember vision-boarding is not a passive affair. You've been implementing the chapters in your workbook, and I hope you're excited about your beautiful visual. Good job action-taker!

Workbook Actionable

Enjoy ticking off the action steps. Then place your inspiring board in a prominent place where you can see it often. (Daily if possible)

7 - Step Vision Board Creation Checklist

1. Desire: I have spent time with the Dream Giver and gotten His vision for me.

2. Define: I have physically written down the vision I received internally.

3. Determine: I have considered and chosen the format of my visual.

4. Develop: I have created my beautiful, inspiring board.

5. Describe: I have interpreted my visual and silenced the inner critic.

6. Decide: I have MSM goals and have scheduled my next micro-step.

7. Do It: I have committed to the law of action and Kaizen-ing my vision daily.

CHAPTER 6

WHY SOME VISION BOARDS DON'T WORK

"Indeed, this life is a test. It is a test of many things - of our convictions and priorities, our faith and our faithfulness, our patience and our resilience, and in the end, our ultimate desires." - Sheri L. Dew

Some possible reasons for vision board failures are:

1. Idolatry and covetousness

"And He said to them,"Take heed and beware of covetousness, for one's life does not consist in the abundance of the things he possesses."
- Luke 12:15

If the given vision becomes more important than the Giver; we have a problem. The Merriam dictionary defines covetousness as: *"Having a craving or an inordinate desire for wealth, possessions or for another's possessions."* Idolatry is anything that we make more important than God. Sometimes this can be very subtle.

Solution: A simple spot test to check idolatry levels is to ask yourself how much of your time, resources and energy do you dedicate to your dreams and desires in comparison to time with God?

2. Lack of grit and patience

Wikipedia describes grit as: *"A trait based on an individual's passion for a particular long-term goal or end state, coupled with a powerful motivation to achieve their respective objective."*

There are no microwave successes, and significant things take time. Yet many people give up on their dreams shortly before manifestation. Though the vision may tarry, don't get too fixated on when something will happen. Trust the process and always be open to course correct as you feel led. We need Godly wisdom to know when to get off a dead horse.

Solution: Exercise patience. God is more interested in our character than our happiness. Often we have to grow into the person who manifests the vision. Be persistent but not too attached to a particular process or outcome. If one dream dies, go back to the ask-and-listen stage and get a new one.

3. Lack of corresponding action and support

"The vision must be followed by the venture. It is not enough to stare up the steps - we must step up the stairs." - Vance Havner

This one is similar to the *Do It Daily* step with the additional point of trying to build the dream all by yourself. Successful people are proactive. They turn their dreams into goals with plans, then they get to executing. A common trait among them is knowing the success journey is not for lone rangers.

There are no rich hermits. It takes teamwork to make the dream work, so look for and connect with like-minded people. Find a coach or mentor – paid or unpaid. Seek the support and guidance you need.

Remember to acknowledge the Giver of the vision and your biggest supporter - God. He knows the best route to where you want to go. He knows the people who will be a good fit for you, whether it's friends, marriage partners, clients, mentors, or coaches. He also knows ahead of time the folks that can cause you grief and stress. The ones that have the potential to knowingly, or unknowingly derail you from His purpose and destiny.

Instead of looking to people as your source, trust your heavenly Father to provide the resources you need to build the dream He gave you. Because when He gives a vision, He also makes provision; *"And the Lord will guide you continually, and satisfy you with all good things, and keep you healthy too; and you will be like a well-watered garden, like an everflowing spring."* TLB (Isaiah 58:11)

As a fellow creative visionary, I know from experience sometimes we get excited about ideas and quickly run off to do our own thing. I've often found myself asking God to bless *my* plans, instead of getting *His* blessed plans. But if we ask for help and wisdom, then acknowledge Him in all our ways, He'll show us the best way to achieve the dream.

There's a spiritual and natural side to vision boarding. And both sides involve faith, common sense, and work. Get support, and a plan of action, then implement and track daily. You can have the best idea, but nothing happens until action is taken.

To wrap up allow me to expound on the corresponding action point. Living in Germany for almost 20 years has significantly contributed to how I plan and take calculated risks. Compared to my motherland, Kenya - East Africa, where we are pretty easy-going and spontaneous, Germans are very efficient and thorough. When they do something, they deliver quality.

But first, they assess, then plan.

And plan.

Get data, then plan.

Test, and plan some more.

Before any action is taken, you can be sure multiple people have thought things through. On all kinds of levels.

Thoroughly.

With all kinds of data.

And paperwork.

And laws. Which ensures quality and order.

A standard way to greet someone in German is by asking *"Alles in Ordnung?"* - *Is everything in order?*

Or, *"Alles klar?"* - *Is everything clear?*

Laws, systems, and order is their thing. Even with greetings. Which is in and of itself not a bad thing.

But the flip side is they have way too much red-tape and bureaucracy. Unlike back in Kenya where we often wing it, and self-initiatives are encouraged, sometimes the bureaucracy, and excessive analyzing hampers creativity and Start-Ups in Germany.

Despite this cultural differences I try to make the best of both worlds; planning *and* spontaneous action. All the while keeping the faith aspect front and center by acknowledging the Dream Giver as I move along. Faith and action a twins.

Solution: Instead of allowing inertia to set in because of bureaucracy, over-planing, analysis paralysis and stalling as you wonder whether you're in God's will or not, take micro steps of faith. Acknowledging Him is a matter of the heart, and He knows our motives. If your heart is right and you're going down the wrong path, He knows how to find you and help you course-correct.

I said it before, but it's worth repeating - you can not steer a parked car. For God to guide and lead you, you have to be moving even when everything is not German *klar*. Keep taking action. Figure things out and tweak as you go.

Done is better than perfect so get support, and accountability because they 'll help you stay in motion as you activate your dreams.

Workbook Actionable

Because working on your vision is a personal process, it's advisable to regularly ask God if there's any way you may unknowingly be sabotaging your dreams. If something doesn't seem right or you have no peace about an action step, journal about it. Think on paper and pray.

If the Dream-Giver shows you something that's not in order, as the Germans would say, "*Nicht In Ordnung*," ask Him for the solution and wisdom to course-correct. Then keep moving.

CONCLUSION

ENJOY THE JOURNEY!

"Vision without action is merely a dream. Action without vision just passes the time. Vision with action can change the world." - Joel A. Barker

Congratulations on creating your vision board and finishing this book! To wrap up, I'd like to encourage you to keep in mind that activating your dreams is a process. God told Habakkuk *the vision would tarry (delay). But we're to wait for it because at the appointed time, it will surely come.* The appointed time of manifestation can be days, weeks, months, years or a lifetime.

Like a journey that has many steps, vision boarding is just a step towards living by design, following your purpose and achieving success. As you determine your daily actions, have fun, be flexible, and keep the faith.

Here are some conclusive tips to remember about your journey:

1. Dream big! We have a big God. His plans and purposes as so much bigger and better than some of the tiny dreams we cling to. As someone said, *"If your dreams don't scare you, they're too small."*

Ideally, your vision board will include something you know you can't quickly achieve in a few weeks or months on your own. Something that will stretch you and your faith.

2. Own your vision unapologetically. Just as your fingerprint is unique, so too are the dreams God gives you. Don't fall into the comparison trap, or try to imitate others. You're an original, and God has a unique path and purpose for you. Embrace it with passion and zeal.

3. There is no right or wrong way to activate your dreams. Be flexible and remember a vision board is just a visual to inspire you. It is not the compass for your life. Rely on the Holy Spirit's leading and let God's powerful promises be the foundation you build on. Know that *"He who began a good work in you, He will complete it."* (Philippians 1:6)

4. Faith and patience. The turbo twins you need for the long haul. More often than not, dreams take longer to manifest than we care to wait. But *"Don´t grow weary in well doing for in due season you will reap if you faint not."* (Galatians 6:9) God's due season is always later than ours. Though the vision may tarry, wait and trust His timing.

5. Instead of getting attached to specific results, enjoy the journey. Obsessing over the outcome is not advisable. God may have a grander plan. Pray and trust the process even when things look like they're not going as you anticipated. Let Jesus be the *Author and Finisher of your faith.* (Hebrews 12:2)

6. *"Trust in the Lord with all your heart, and lean not on your own understanding; In all your ways*

acknowledge Him, and He shall direct your paths." (Prov. 3:5-6) As you do this, may *"He give you the desires of your heart and make all your plans succeed."* (Psalm 20:4)

7. As you walk by faith and grow into your vision, the person you became in Christ is way more important than what you acquire or achieve. (Ephesians 2:20) Just like we started this book with a prayer, finish by committing your dreams and future plans to God in prayer. Get support, and embrace the concept of growing into your full potential. Believe *you can do all things, through Christ who strengthens you.* (Philippians 4:13)

VISION BOARDING CHECKLIST

- ✓ I have downloaded my free workbook + video training
- ✓ I have taken quiet time to listen to the Dream-Giver
- ✓ I have allowed myself to dream and envision about my core areas:
  - ○ Faith & Fulfillment
  - ○ Fitness & Health
  - ○ Family & Friends
  - ○ Finances & Business
  - ○ Fun & Self-Care
  - ○ Future & Legacy
- ✓ I have written down my vision statement
- ✓ I have done my *Wheel of Balance* assessment
- ✓ I have determined the format of my vision board
  - ○ Physical
  - ○ Digital
- ✓ I have gathered the necessary materials
- ✓ Cork / bulletin / whiteboard, frame or book
- ✓ Construction paper, binder or folder
- ✓ Magazines and books or images from (Pinterest /Google)
- ✓ Pins, magnets (or clipboard for digital)
- ✓ Scissors, glue, and tape
- ✓ Colored pens or pencils

- ✓ I have cut out images that speak to me from magazines and books
- ✓ I have organized my materials into categories that match my vision boards
- ✓ I have created a beautiful vision board that inspires me
- ✓ I have done some mindset work and described my vision board
- ✓ I have posted my vision board in a prominent place for daily inspiration
- ✓ I have decided what step to take next
- ✓ I have done a quick spot-check for potential vision board failure
- ✓ I have located paid or free options to get accountability and support
- ✓ I will schedule times to revisit my vision board to see if it still inspires and makes me happy.
- ✓ I have committed my future plans and actions to God in prayer.

I, ...(Name) by the grace and wisdom of God, commit to mixing faith with action by doing something daily (micro, small, or medium) to activate and achieve my God-given dreams.

Signed......................................

Date: ...../........../20.....

Prayer of Salvation

"Heavenly Father, I come to You in the Name of Jesus. Your Word says, *"Whosoever shall call on the name of the Lord shall be saved"* (Acts 2:21). I am calling on you and ask you to forgive me of all my sins.

I pray and ask Jesus to come into my heart and be Lord over my life according to Romans 10: 9-10 (NIV) *"That if you confess with your mouth, "Jesus is Lord," and believe in your heart that God raised him from the dead, you will be saved. For it is with your heart that you believe and are justified, and it is with your mouth that you confess and are saved."*

I do that now. I confess that Jesus is Lord, and I believe in my heart that God raised Him from the dead. I thank you that I am now saved. A born-again Christian. Amen.!

***

If you prayed and made this important life-changing decision, you've begun an exciting journey of faith. I encourage you to find a church with believers who help you can grow. I'd also love to hear from you. Please write or e-mail me so that I can celebrate with you. Write to:

Nancy Gathecha
Postfach 7586
53075
Bonn, Germany

www.NancyGathecha.com

ABOUT THE AUTHOR

Nancy Gathecha is a Kenyan author, speaker, digital consultant and podcast producer based in Germany.

She loves inspiring people on the topics of faith, vision, and success by design - so that they enjoy a life of purpose, passion, and profits.

As a speaker and trainer she helps people achieve their goals. And as a consultant shows companies how to increase revenue using digital marketing strategies.

To hire Nancy as a consultant, coach or speaker for your event, please visit,
www.NancyGathecha.com

RECOMMENDED RESOURCES AND PRODUCTS RELATED TO THIS BOOK

Bonus Workbook + Video
www.DesignYourVisionBoard.com

Goals eCourse
(20% discount code inside the workbook)

eCourses
www.DesignYourSuccessAcademy.com
(DYSAcademy.com)

Podcast
www.DesignYourSuccessPodcast.com
(www.DYSPodcast.com)

Get Free Resources
www.nagatips.com

Nancy offers ala cart product creation and publishing services for print books and digital products.

For all your publishing and product creation queries, please visit www.DigitalProductsProfits.com

Made in the USA
Lexington, KY
25 March 2019